NUTLEY POND

Lyn Lifshin

D1548108

Goose River Press
Waldoboro, Maine

Library of Congress Card Number: 2008926794

ISBN 13: 978-1-59713-068-4

First Printing, 2008

Published by
Goose River Press
3400 Friendship Road
Waldoboro ME 04572
e-mail: gooseriverpress@roadrunner.com
www.gooseriverpress.com

INTRODUCTION TO NUTLEY POND

When I first moved to Nutley Pond, the houses were brand new, trees so scraggly water seemed as close as the next room. That first day, while I was unpacking, I was astonished at a flotilla of geese floating past. They were gorgeous. I had never seen anything wild so close. In Vermont I grew up over a loud waterfall too furious and loud for much but froth and ragged branches. Animals and birds would have been washed away.

Now, years later, the maples gnawed by beavers the first Christmas morning, along with pines and cherry bark, have spread. You can see the pond only in patches beyond the flaming maples this November morning. It's half hidden, the way it is with the brilliant pink blossoms and lush summer leaves: jade that has taken over where deer leaped and raccoons and a fox trotted close to my stairs. The forest has morphed to brick condos. Those sticks of cherry and apple trees cover the shore, flourish along with fragrant wild plum with their wine leaves. Late February I often cut a branch or two to bring into the house to bloom. But the close up streaks of glistening gold fish under the surface of Nutley Pond, that shimmering gold and guava, are hidden by maples, willows, pines and hemlock. Our "video cam" of the goslings and ducklings with their antics I gazed at, felt soothed by, are lost in emerald. Muskrat, deer, raccoons seem more rare while the reeds and cat tails spread along with swamp rose, blue flag, sedge and frogs and squirrels.

But those first years, the pond with its herons and ducks and gulls felt like another room you could just walk into. Feathers were on the deck like strange hieroglyphs. Even as I wrote about the pond, wrote about the birds and plants and animals living there, I imagined mysterious half bird, half women creatures, imagined their tracks in the sand told amazing stories, could almost hear Leda-like women calling. Those poems are unlike all my others.

But these poems are of the pond life I watched, photographed and drew. One year I bought 600 lbs of corn, half slid thru snow and ice and once at least was close to slipping into the icy water as if I wanted to join the birds. Alone in the house, I felt less alone listening to their harsh serenade near midnight. Walking back from the metro, past the pond, they kept me company. I imagined they recognized my voice and swam close to the path with me. Some people complained of the mess the geese made. I was enchanted. The death of one duck or goose darkened the hours.

When The Washington Post interviewed me for a feature article (www.lynlifshin.com) they came to the pond for a series of photographs. Several are of me with the geese in the article published in The Washington Post Magazine article by Mary Batiatta, " Madonna who Writes Ten Poems a Day." Huge screens of light were set up on the shore of the pond like drive in movie screens. Neighbors rushed out to look as one spring one neighbor did after a storm when a raft of tiny ducklings were washed over the dam. He came back soaked with several of the small ducks in his arms. One warm apple blossom scented May night I watched eight to twelve goslings move under the mother goose who spread out on the grass to let the babies move in under her feather skirt like Mother Ginger in the Nutcracker, hiding her ginger babies in the folds of her skirt.

As calming as that May night was, another, a winter evening was devastating. I heard shots in the night and in the morning, mid- pond on the ice, saw the still, life-less shape. It took a second look to recognize the rounded shape the color of the snowy ice. The dead goose was haunting. For a few days, tracks, so many they erased each other circled the carcass as what was once alive sunk into itself, its flesh carried off into the night until there was only a faint red smear, some feathers. Finally snow covered where the plundered goose had been.

Sun rise is over the pond. I've photographed the brilliant rubies, garnets, turquoise, tangerines, sapphires and violets. Some winters hoards of geese huddle on the ice as if certain spots were a heating pad. In summers, feathers from the molting make Nutley Pond look snow glazed. The willows, cherries, pear and peach, exotic as I imagine Monet's pallet.

One day I noticed a bird with a band on it's neck and I jotted the day down, the time and hour it came and went. Then another banded bird came. Someone told me it was nothing, probably just to show there were too many geese. I tried to read more about wild birds but didn't find that much. When FLY AWAY HOME, the film about the sculptor-inventor Bill Lishman teaching motherless geese to migrate following an ultra light plane came out, I wanted to see it. I had read an article about this experiment and thought it was fascinating. A few days after the movie, The Washington Post had an article about the "real life" science behind the film with Dr William Sladen (who runs Operation Migration). There were photographs of some of the geese he had trained and news of his plans to work to bring endangered swans to the Chesapeake. I wasn't sure where Airlie Center was, just that it was in Virginia. I did, though, notice the bands on the geese in the newspaper looked familiar. Checking it out (amazed I could actually find the notes I had taken,) I realized the numbers on the metal "neck bracelets" were close. My goose was K721. I wrote Dr Sladen, wondered if he gave lectures, could recommend some books. A few days later, my phone began ringing non stop. Biologists, environmentalists called to beg me to call back at any time of the day or night.

It turned out my goose was a treasure: I had seen one of the original geese from Lishman and Sladen's experiment. I'm not sure how well everyone knows his story but between the film and his book Father Goose as well as some appearances on places like 20/20, his touching story of teaching motherless geese to follow his ultra-light plane has intrigued many people. He and Dr. Sladen raised the tiny goslings and began to train them to survive on their own. Of those 15 geese they taught to follow the light plane from Canada, over New York and Maryland and Virginia, and then on to North Carolina, 13 of the 15 geese were never seen in United States after five days in North Carolina. They returned to Canada. "My goose" came back separately. But no one had seen any of the geese in this country. I was the only person to see her. I met Lishman, who picked out a drawing of one of the geese in his book and autographed it to me, sure it was K721! The records show it was a female. I watched for her return. I like to think I wrote her into my life, that the goose poems grew and then she became real. Though I never saw her again, I am hoping some of the new goslings each year are her descendants. From the start I knew this bird was special, much tamer than other geese. She would eat out of my hand. Even before I knew anything about her I sensed she was somehow apart from the other geese, flying with them but on her own and in her own world.

This morning, a strange noise, very much like what I heard once before finding five or six geese perched on the roof. The geese, a jazzy riff in the spring and fall and then like a long pause in music, subdued, silent when they molt. Sometimes the music from the pond twisted into dreams: heron screech, shrews, duck calls, crows, crickets. Sometimes fierce animal noises split the quiet. What better afternoon break then to just listen to the sounds: the wood duck calling her hatchlings back, dragon flies' whirring music. Birds I'll never know the names of rustle leaves. Even in summer, the sound of water, a dark whisper through pale wet stones and the crickets louder, then silent

And the smells: leaf scent, wet wood, mud and dried thistles, pine. The water's surface a kaleidoscope. A silt island is growing. Each season, different gifts. Lilies break up from murky shale crowding the black lace. Egrets with their bamboo legs, lashes of willow polishing the water. Wait a little and a muskrat will swim thru pads and grass, leave a white foam. Some nights waiting for northern lights it's as if the pond tossed the stars and moon up like fire crackers.

Brown and muddy after storms, it's hard with all the leaves to imagine that glint of gold fish moving like yards of silk. Frozen in snow, mallards and snow geese, white on white, move as if in their own dreams. Hard to imagine stars swimming in blue black ripples when the pond opens. When I can't sleep, I should think of floating on the pond among milky stars. When I can't sleep I should imagine drifting thru the lilies, imagine those gold fins and scales glistening on my body. If I leave the windows open, I can imagine creatures you never see in the light. Though I never have, I dream of sleeping as close to the pond as my lips are to my fingers. Today in November, late fall, everything shifts. Uneaten nuts crumble in dampness. The last of the late rose flutters east. The maple is blazing, this last flare of life before it lets go of what astonishes and the pond comes back

WINTER: In the Rippled Ebony Cove

FIELDS SMOLDER WITH LIGHT

Temperatures falling.
Moon slivers on the
rolling skin of water.
Geese in half light,
armada of feathers.
Wind blows them closer.
One silver band glows.
  Their onyx, black flame
in a night fire

IN THE ONE SPACE THAT WASN'T FROZEN

the heron, deep
in pond water,
still as sticks

and then, a sudden
swoop like the
last fruit falling

off a tree into snow.
I happened to see it,
standing near the

window, that flash
of tangerine and
gold in its beak like

a barb of sun, a slice
of orange in colorless
air. It's been so long

I don't remember
something I looked for
and wanted to come

came so fast

HERON ON ICE

Pale salmon light,
9 degrees. Floor
tiles icy. Past
branches the
beaver's gnawed

at the small hole
the heron waits,
deep in the water.
Sky goes apricot,
tangerine, rose.

Suddenly, a dive,
then the heron
with sun squirming
in his mouth, a
carp that looks a

third as big as he
is gulped, then
swallowed, orange
glittering wildly
like a flag or the

wave of someone
drowning

GEESE ON ICE

frozen, perched as
if listening for some
distant code,
news of a warm

front coming in
time. Meanwhile,
alerts go out on
local stations,

schools close
early. The "partly
sunny" never came.
30 percent chance

of snow. Trees tilt
east, the ground
hardens. Geese
take root as scarves

float in wind like
strange new flags

BEFORE ANY SNOW

you can taste it.
Before trees
glitter, a heavy
dampness after
Indian Summer.
Air's a wet
blanket. Two
sweat shirts
aren't enough.
The gulls seem
oblivious, flap up
from across the
pond where I shiver
thru soggy grass,
descend, fifty
parachutes of feathers
skidding on pewter
glass

THE WILLOWS

have merged with
plum and cherry
in a white lilac
sky. Velvet snow,

a Monet's snow.
Midnight. Past the
equinox, blackness
still coats the stairs.

Brown rose, each
petal, powdered,
slate going talc.
Tracks going away

from the house
gulped as you
stand there

AS BRANCHES CLATTER

and iced limbs crack
something inside seems
as vulnerable, precarious,
a darkness I can't even
name though I feel its
beak and claws pull
fear from where it
was and bring it back
to where I live like that
bird, the one I hear
so many midnights
that pulls a thread
from leaves of flowers
and with its beak
sews what wasn't
into his house

TRYING TO JUST SMELL THE TANGERINE TREE'S BLOSSOMS

the light going,
muskrats slither
toward damp stones

gold ripples
under the pond's
pewter days from

the day of the
shortest light.
Small animals

under tawny dead
reeds and lilies,

cradles of burnt sienna
as black closes in

WALKING PAST THE POND AT NIGHT

December,
record
breaking
warm. Geese
in clumps,
opalescent
under this
copper moon.
Mist, a
blue heron.
Edges slide
together,
darkness wraps
my hair like
a scarf
of stars

DECEMBER POND

The v of mallards
criss-crosses the
beaver's wake.
Snow silence.
Feathers clot on
apricot water.
Dried camellias
flutter like the
feathers. What
isn't, haunts like
the name "Bethany"
or the stain on
a quilt that some
how sucks me back
to before my mother
was howling in the
smallest dark room
under a moon
of brass

THIS DECEMBER

it's almost 70
after dark.
I stop by the pond
instead of
shivering back.
Shapes in clumps
like tumbleweeds
floating on
some prairie,
the moon in haze
dazzling as
pale teeth of cats.
Silver light, a
blaze of willow.
Lights from the
metro, rhinestones
thru trees,
branches of stars

BEFORE THE BEAVER SLITS PEWTER'S SILK

this warm spell
with dandelions
in bloom, a coppery
glow thru dark
cotton. Walking
thru bleached grass,
light rose as cats'
feet. In a breath,
buttery lemon sun,
crows wild as
hands on fire,
black ducks floating
on silk and stars

THURSDAY, WALKING PAST THE POND
NEAR MIDNIGHT

willow roots, grass clumped
with feathers. No geese until
you look long enough to

see them floating like pale
cotton batten or spun sugar.
Hickory nuts on creosote.

Without leaves, lights from
the metro blaze, yellow
diamonds bathing the hill

THE POND ON THE WALK BACK FROM THE METRO, DECEMBER, A NIGHT YOU CAN SMELL THE MELT

without leaves,
lights thru silver
branches hang
icicle stars.
Jade and ruby
lights. I think of
Liv Ullman saying
"life is what goes
on in other people's
rooms." Squishy
earth, barberry.
New dandelions.
Birds in clumps.
Feathers on the
silk of the pond
like ghosts about to
take the shape of
whatever you
make of them

GEESE FLOATING

after the December
night it stays in
the 60's, the pond
a plate of grey,
jade and ruby,
flashing lights
on grey brocade.
After it's too
warm for a parka
the geese float,
tumbleweeds of
feathers drifting
thru reeds

EARLY, 20 DEGREES, JANUARY

wood's almost white
before water goes
rose. What's left
of night pools in
coves. Black ripples.
Indigo outlines. A
slate V. Ice tipped
feathers. Dark flickers
as melon spreads,
breath, a caption
anything, still could
be written on. A
doe dimpling
new snow

SLATE INDIGO, THE COLDEST JANUARY MORNING

iced grass
goose droppings
go stone in.
Pewter tinged ice.
Guava streaks.
Rain water's crystal.
A blue shoe,
glazed. Light
slicks over the pond,
past paper stuffed
into the hole under
the porch shredded
this morning to a nest
for something that
moves in close
thru the dark

ANOTHER RECORD BREAKING JANUARY DAY

the heron, in the only patch
of water that's not frozen.
hard earth, not even a
blanket of snow. No
color in he sky. Someone

says a storm is coming.
The heron waits, patient
as the reeds, the same
color, oblivious to wind
and cars, then, quick as

a sneeze, plunges into
water like dunking a
croissant in coffee, jerks
back up: the only color
in the pewter landscape.

A huge gold-orange fish
wriggles, twitches
then is gulped like
a lover's tongue.

JANUARY 11

if there was snow
raccoons would be

foraging thru
snow banks,

the stones by the
pond buried, mounds

big as cows.
Rain jewels on

the tree a
nest hangs on

tight in the black
branch's crotch,

invisible in
whiteness.

Footsteps, missteps,
what nobody wanted

under the
white roof of sleep

JANUARY 14

each branch
wet jeweled,

crystalline,
pellucid. There

will be no
moon hurrying

in blackness
past the pond,

no candles, moon,
glitter of ribbons.

The geese huddled
in thickets, fog

camouflaging

what I wish
I could

FROM THE PORCH BEFORE IT'S LIGHT

mist smokes up
from the pond.
Car lights, a
string of rubies,
garnets. Steam
camouflages
roots. Maples
seem about to
float up out of
the moon in the
ripples as if
everywhere we
stand was once
water and we
are floating again

HONKING THE LIGHT BACK: SPRING

AT THE POND EARLY

night grass steams.
Mourning doves in
the fog, a few feathers

on the lawn though no
geese for two days.
Only the heron like

a slate candle, a drift
wood stick and my
17 year old cat, a

cloth mouse in her
jaws muffling a shriek,
cuts the sleeve

of quiet

ON THE AFTERNOON THE GEESE COME

you can smell ice
breaking up, scent
of watercress uncurling.
Only a few months
from the longest
dark day, willows
fling blond tentacles.
Wet clay smells
sweeter. In blackness
past the metro last
night, a fingernail
moon. Some say it
smells wilder than
a full moon, that
herons listening for fish
under the pond's crust
can smell dreams of
anything moving

GEESE AT MIDNIGHT

as if honking the
light back thru
the pine's lashes

like women floating
barefoot into fields
starved for some moon,

their white wings
on blue wood, a rustle
in wetness. This

was not a dream though
it held me as close

THAW

all night, the ice
shoves. The pond,
a dark blossom
unfolding,
camouflaged.
White thru blinds,
feathers or white
lilies suspended
instead of moon.
Fog lips on
roots and willows
filtering into
dreams of swans
scooping to
crusts, braiding
wings and thighs

FROM THE PORCH IN THE STILL ALMOST DARK

before plum and flesh twitch
across the pond and only
the palest lemon skitters
blackness, a v of froth,
black embroidery
on wild birds, blazing,
leaving a white wake
you see before you see
them, small rafts of
feathers on a dark linen
silver and lavender
move into, the light
polishing water,
connecting what was
behind to what's ahead

APRIL FOG

The wind picks up
the day it's supposed
to rise into the
upper sixties. Clouds

boil. The pond goes
pewter. Ripples dark
as basaltic lava.
You can measure light

by what's gone,
throwing corn
past crushed berries,
the only light and the

bellies of geese
tipped to dive
for those
gold beads

GEESE EARLY

slanting back
from their night pond,
before any gold or apricot
blossoms on the water.

The plate of the moon
still on the lake's skin.
After the mallards,
their jade the only

glimmer in shadow,
the geese glide,
skid on dark silk
to honk sun back

MARCH 20

After weeks in the
80's, after cherry
boughs explode in
pale rose two weeks
early, the almost
white white against
a milk sky. After
shivering past
people in parkas
trying to eat lunch
under the gnarled
bark or holding
three dogs in
blankets or in
hoods, the wind
kicking up, colder
than on New
Year's Eve Day.
After the cat coils
into her cloth
snake, her muff
on the bed and I'm
shivering in three
sweatshirts, I
turn the heat up,
chartreuse creeping
in slower near
the pond these
last icy days,

Continued

stalling like a
woman who was
wild to open
suddenly pulling
her legs together.
The daffodils
on the bank go
into fists, a cold
front, a hush of
ice. The pear
branches' snow
could be snow

APRIL

yes, the loveliest,
a smudge of rouge
lips blotted against
dark boughs. Only
the pear and magnolia
ahead of the cherries'
blush lace, almost
a haze, almost a no
blossom snow any
storm could send
swirling so by the
morning the pond
would have a skin
of rose, the trees
bare with just a fuzz
of green shaking

BEFORE THE POND IS LIGHT

the blossoms glow
like stars of lace,
heavy snow
clotting on boughs.
I couldn't sleep,
the sweet white
floating up
from Nutley's shore
pulled me back
to an old lover's
arms, deep in
such white
dripping branches,
white petals
on slopes of
skin, lips
studding Monday
with jewels
in the sweet
grass, locked
like antlers

THIS GLOW OF WHITE BRANCHES

clots of snow,
stars in clumps.
Past the pond
you have to bury
your face in
white. Other
Aprils, the
lilacs just
starting, the
first man who
touched me
inside my
clothes pulled
me under such
white boughs
thru dripping rain.
Lacy boughs,
a glow filling
that orchard.
In this same
jeweled light
everything
opening like
these clenched buds

SUMMER: a Wind of White Rose Petals

AS IF A FEATHER

quilt exploded,
a white you can't
see in the dark
but breathe, a
wind of white
rose petals,
a wave of fog
in the shape of
flying things.
Like radio
voices on
the pillow,
lulling, keeping
what's ragged
and tears at
bay, the geese
pull sky and stars
in thru glass,
are like arms,
coming back
as sound

BEFORE ANY LAVENDER STREAKS,
THE BLACK POND

maple tea, I'm still
in flannel pajamas
I haven't worn since
high school. Summer
school buses stream
by. A cold spell in
summer. Sometimes I
think blackness
remembers me, takes
me back, soft as
this down quilt. This
darkness will rearrange
her licorice raglan
sleeves and promise
a sleep I can drown in,
half heavy goose
music, half owls near
the pond: night music,
the birds that do what
they do in darkness
so I can wake up to
write a poem of light
in this blackness

ALL NIGHT THE GEESE

float in marsh
grass, pale shapes,
pewter stones on
water's skin. Only
the v of white
where they tip
noiselessly
in past ripples.
Goldfish glow like
opals. The geese
float like ghost
ships, soundless,
past ferns and
goldenrod, as
if made of mist
as black silk
parts under them

AN ARMADA OF PEWTER SHAPES

moving in darkness,
about to slip
close to shore.
Camouflaged in
shadow, you can't
see anything at
first. Then, the
moon's tongue
licks the only
thing moving on
the skin of water.
Geese glide through
weeds, the world
of fish below them,
slick and noise-
less, trailing
feathers as the
pond's silk ripples

OVER THE SILKY BLACK

like dead moving
into a dream.

Only the moon's
lips, a silver
tongue. The gulls

glide, seem to
float in their
sleep past brown

roses, their
shapes pale as
bone, the

only flash of
white in darkness

LIKE A RADIO ON ALL NIGHT

There, in the dark.
You can't touch
what's closer than
the sheets but a
presence wraps you
closer. It was after
12 when their wings
and honks stirred
the pond. A skid
of webs, flutter
in black silence.
The moon revealed
nothing. I shut the
light off, floated
under blankets like
eel grass, the radio
low, waiting for their
cries like a woman
listening for a child
in the next room

NIGHT SOUNDS FROM THE POND

mysterious as voices
on a radio humming
all night. Some station
blurs and then another
comes in louder. Shapes
in dreams. But the geese
wake me. The moon
uses the blue wood
for a sun dial.
Lights in the room
only blacken what is
already so I watch
in darkness. Feathers
float over the water, a
flutter as close as voices
on the air whose
stories make a cove

LIKE SOMEONE REELING IN A

line in darkness, the
moon turns wet grass
to a sundial. I'm
pulled to the geese,
their honks and feathers
in blackness. The digital
clock bleeps 12:04.
They must have been
starved, or couldn't
sleep like voices
calling a talk show until
morning, soothing as
the shape of the cat
against my hip, the
breath of someone who
matters. The radio
keeps bad dreams at
bay like a magnetic
field. The geese
move in waves,
Their feathers,
rose petals in hail

THOSE STATIONS FLICKERING IN AND OUT

that tide washing
out bad dreams.
Bird sounds after
midnight like chocolates
on the spread or the
iridescent shell
something dying
wriggled out of,
left as a last
word the moon
picks up and spits
out like Braille.
Honking in darkness,
like some other,
a twin I never
knew sending the
messages in a
language now I
need to learn.
In the light,
you'd suppose
their wings,
phantoms,
dissolving like a
man who leaves in
the night as white
feathers drift
in, cover the pond,
the reeds, the porch

BEFORE PEWTER BRAIDS WITH ROSE

and frogs and
newts sleep
under willows.
Before beavers
slit the scrim of
water, the geese
float, sleep
walkers in mist,
a drifting slope
of pillows. They
don't touch,
still as canoes, a
plane feathering
its engines, moon
dazed phantoms
on silk currents

EVEN AFTER PEWTER IS

tinged with rouge,
black mallards
move on the
watery quilt.
Ovals of feathers
drift, a train of
sleepers or
pale shadowy
stones of air,
ghosts of white
flowers on
water about to
become the
shape of
what holds it

BEFORE BEAVERS

slit the flesh
of the pond,
water animals
float, ghosts
in mist still
as reflections
of the willows.
Their pale
yellow spreads
over dark
grass like
long hair
cradling a
woman lost
in sleep's lilies

SUMMER NIGHT NEAR THE POND

not targeting corn
or churning ripples.
Not a sound. The
birds float as if
stunned or amazed
as the current takes
them into the cove
pink lipstick light
starts to fade in.
Sleeping, floating.
White clouds of
doves. Owls.
Faces in dreams.
Ghosts you
could walk thru

HUMMOCKS OF FEATHERS ON THE POND

huge mounds on water
the color of their
shape, the swans
float as on a train
made of water, move
like subway sleepers
half hearing stations,
destinations tattooed
in their blood

MUSKRATS SKITTER DOWN TO THE POND

before any
lavender or
mauve, before
silver on
branches seems
a sequin fire,
a dew fills
the reeds on
shore. Dragon
flies hover,
float on stars

PAST SOGGY GRASS

red sand. Bronze
mounds lose
their tops in mist.
Moths and bees
clot, hidden
under the oak
leaves. Geraniums,
the only color
as outlines blur,
edges sliding
into each other.
Marsh grass.
Pond lilies, ferns.
Every thing you can
touch glitters
with rain

MARSH FLOWERS

budding out
of shadows.
Each year the
green thickens.
Snakes, moths,
butterflies and
water lilies.
Fox slither past
climbing jasmine,
past the angel
trumpet tree.
At every tip
of earth, a
word you can't
decipher, memory
of when every
thing that
breathed under
water was
like fish so old
they had no eyes,
every deer
print a
hieroglyph

FIRST QUIET MORNING, AUGUST

after a night
floating from
the black river
the moon clots
in feathers.
Before the
geese and
heat that
bleaches white
from wood,
honey clots on
the counter,
smells of clover
and a trail
of sweetness
like Gretle left
in trees or long
strands of hair
pasted into an
envelope to a
stranger for
him to follow

FALL: Ruby Oaks,
the Coming Blue Sack of Cold

SEPTEMBER 24

this morning the pond
looks like marble. Rose
and charcoal dissolving
to dove, to flesh, rouge.
Only mallards pushing
holes in the glass, so
unlike that pond, deep in
trees, almost camouflaged,
startling as coming upon
your reflection in a mirror,
just there under trees and
the wooden bar and the
driftwood benches blackly
jade with pines dripping
into it, shadows close to
my hair. What I didn't have
blinded me so I hardly saw
the small birds, blue
pulling out of moss and
needles as if reaching into
the dark for their color

AT THE END OF SEPTEMBER

the lawn chair's red
wood is bleached to
rouge. Only the
new maples go
brighter, a scarlet
drifting to clover.
Crickets come indoors,
coil in bags of cracked
corn, black shapes
that sprint behind shelves.
Webs braid across a
door you open less
and less as if the
cold grass couldn't
still support you

BRISTLES OF LIGHT STICKING UP
OUT OF THE EAST

after the moon set,
six pale shapes
on the black polished
water. Ovals float
on lemon capped
ripples, slosh on
shore. Mallards float,
flickering sticks
on water. Willow
lashes dip into
plates of fire. Ghosts
lurch slow motion
past corn, move
as if under water
or in amber

AFTER THE MOON ROSE

after lights went
out in back yards and
porches, after the
blossom of the rising
moon was sliced by
branches, pale
shapes, almost a
mirage, almost
a part of the brown
dying lilies, the
birds float
slow motion to
where a shape as
blurred maybe to them
flings bread in blackness

GLIDING FROM THE MIDDLE OF THE POND

ghost boats,
beads of night
out past weeds
and blood oak.
Nights near the
bank watching
an eclipse,
northern lights.
The glow out-
lines slopes.
Only a muffled
honk like a
truck backing
up. Then just
night water as
the birds move
into the lilies,
slither thru brown
roses of sleep

A GHOST ARMADA

mirage from mallow
flowers and pickerel
weed moving closer
to the edge from
murky shales.
Soundless. You
could imagine the
shapes are stones
you can see thru.
White under bellies
move like men
disguised as trees
on to grass, a
shadow, sound
that could be your
skin brushing
against your
own skin

RAIN ALMOST BLURRING NUTLEY POND

green balls on
the tangerine,
torn guava at
the edge. No
dark news yet,
no blues in he
burnt grass
roses drip in.
No space like
a grave in the
air yet, no goat's
head in trees,
no blond hair
on barbwire.
There are no
dreams of the
dead brushing
my hair, only
the softness of
cotton my mother
wore the last
year holding
me loosely
as the pond
laps driftwood.

AFTER THE WARNING OF BLOOD

in the maples,
and afternoon light
is a drug thru black

wool, the first
snow moves east
smelling of icicles.

In a cove of blankets,
the only warmth is
in the shape of

my body, a comma before
white's assault.
Lady bugs are iced

to screens, pale
pond flowers frozen,
bent over like a woman

on her knees whose
summer cotton
isn't enough

LIGHTS FROM THE METRO

after the leaves go,
after thick green
is in piles, ragged
antler branches
lose their heads
in mist until
the weather turns
cool and even clouds
freeze on wires.
Birds huddle in
reeds of ice. Light
comes on in the after
noon, stars you couldn't
see all summer, a
splatter of glitter
in lemon, wild as a
blaze of poems or a
hill sized tree of
flaming candles.
Light sends up
streams of diamond,
fountains of fire,
amber beads caught
in amber flooding
blackness just
weeks from the
longest night

PINK MORNING

rose oak,
the porch is
pink, washed

rose on the water.
Before geese,
the white plastic

chairs go red,
even the mallards
are plum colored

as blush spreads
over the pale rug,
the crotch of trees.

The palest red
as you walk out
into pink snow.

Even corn is the
color of inside
a mouth, a lip, a

tongue, the
lips down
there holding

you in its
softest stain

MUSKRATS SWIMMING THRU THE EDGE OF THE POND'S GRASS

birds singing for light,
for what's gone away
into the earth to hide

the first morning ground
is hard. Feathers braid
with iced grass, slash

grey, a v on pewter, a
split in stone, they
zig zag like a memory

there are not yet
nouns or verbs for,
a shadow of

wings as the
gate opens

LAST STRANDS OF PLUM

and raspberry cling to
the edges, a tapestry
of night. Waves
lap and suck as if
someone opened
the earth and put
back what had come
out of it in darkness
before rain
laps up traces. If
clouds slide out
and the moon lit
up the reflection of
pines glittering on
the skim of water,
you'd just hear night
birds, leaves parting
where deer move
to drink

BEFORE ANY SNOW

before the last
garnet maples slam

from antler branches
and the pond's an
onyx ribbon in white,

black ducks move closer
in thru lapis lazuli
past the apricot

mirror of night,
quaking, clustering
as if lights on the

porch were
bracelets of corn

FEEDING DUCKS AS ICY AIR MOVES IN

after a week of
June in November,
sun thru fleece,
grey moves in
thru maples and
pines. Slate water
only gulls make
ripples in. Damp
grass wind. Mostly
bare branches. By
night it will rain,
the calandria tipped
with jewels calyx
leaves close over.
Only the emerald
shimmer on the
mallards reflects
light you barely see
as edges harden on
shore and tho it's
9 am, I imagine
slithering back under
quilts to let the
coming rain make
dead leaves glitter

SMELL THE LAST

apples in the moon light
knowing someone else
would walk among these
dark apples having
lost what they
were sure they could
never live without.
Not what they'd
been or planned on
becoming, holding
a cold apple
and feeling it
warm as they held it

FEEDING DUCKS, GREY NOVEMBER

no swath of light,
no smell of warm
wood shavings. A
rain coming scent.
Last leaf in wind.
Walnuts on the deck
bleeding ebony. I
think of houses in
ice where there is
no light, of men
carving snow birds,
seals, caribou,
dream llamas as geese
fly up, a cloud of
feathers skidding to
the corn that floats
on the slick of water
the color of light

DEAD GOOSE UNDER BURNT ORANGE LEAVES

after the rain
slammed sideways,
after lights went out
and the other geese
made a bracelet of
themselves until a
streak of salmon light
broke thru and the
pale sun lured them
toward the acorns,
across the green strip
over the body of the
bird gone stone

DEAD GOOSE THE LEAVES DRIFT OVER

still there when I come
back in wild rain, wind
blowing leaves against
where trees have shoved
it, camouflaging the
wound where the head
was. I think of the dead
mole on the art colony
path on its back, pale
belly, feet in the air,
almost human. At 1:30
I heard goose music
from the pond, slow and
deep as a cello in a minor
blue key, music for a
plane crash, mournful
as the stunned family
numb from the news, the
plane ride over the Nile,
Timbuktu, moonless,
starless, dark as the
streak of onyx feathers
glaring thru flame leaves

TRYING TO NOT WRITE A DARK POEM

but to drift, water
that takes the
shape of what
holds it. If I
could sleep, drug-
less as never be-
fore, the stars' white
fire thru blinds,
obsession gulped by
the pond's carp,
at least thru night
where branches
like upside down
roots of trees
glow luminous
against the
Harvest moon

SNOW GEESE

after the last few
burgundy leaves, the
fruit no squirrels
clawed frozen in
grass, mud is a frozen
bracelet. After roots
doze and the moon's
locked behind curtains,
marble cold stag horn
juts like antlers.
Muted blue knives,
slash whiteness
as snow geese
scratch thru silk over
the iced reeds, their
breath insistent
as candles

JANUARY 24

instead of the black leaves,
antler branches.
This morning, a pale swan
delicate as a ballerina
on the pond. Tulle
feathers, wings of white
lilies. The pond,
teal glass as if the night
hadn't been close
to freezing. Sun on water
moves, rearranges
shadows of the bird's body

PURPLE SKY, WINDOWS BLAZING RASPBERRY

you could imagine
rose smoke swirling
from the buildings

Geese slice guava.
A jogger moves
from blackness

Flame trees,
blazing tops
and still in the

crotch of a tree I
don't know the
name of one

nest in the braid of
grass and leaves,
hanging on

into February

About the Author

Lyn has published more than 120 books of poetry, including *Marilyn Monroe, Blue Tattoo*, won awards for her non fiction and edited 4 anthologies of women's writing including *Tangled Vines Ariadne's Thread* and *Lips Unsealed*. Her poems have appeared in most literary and poetry magazines and she is the subject of an award winning documentary film, LYN LIFSHIN: NOT MADE OF GLASS, available from Women Make Movies. Her poem, *No More Apologizing*, has been called among the most impressive documents of the women's poetry movement by Alicia Ostriker.

Lyn Lifshin's *Another Woman Who Looks Like Me* was published by Black Sparrow at David Godine October, 2006. It has been selected for the 2007 Paterson Award for Literary Excellence for previous finalists of the Paterson Poetry Prize. (ORDER@GODINE.COM). Also out in 2006 is her prize winning book about the famous, short lived beautiful race horse, Ruffian: *The Licorice Daughter: My Years With Ruffian* from Texas Review Press.

Other of Lifshin's recent prizewinning books include *Before It's Light* published winter 1999-2000 by Black Sparrow Press, following their publication of *Cold Comfort* in 1997. Other recently published books and chap books include : *In Mirrors* from Presa Press and *Upstate: An Unfinished Story* from Foot

Hills and *The Daughter I Don't Have* from Plan B Press, *When a Cat Dies, Another Woman's Story, Barbie Poems, She Was Last Seen Treading Water,* and *Mad Girl Poems. A New Film About a Woman in Love With the Dead* came from March Street Press in 2003.

An update to her Gale Research Projects Autobiographical series, *On the Outside, Lips, Blues, Blue Lace* was published Spring 2003. *What Matters Most* and *August Wind* were recently published. *Tsunami* is forthcoming from Blue Unicorn. World Parade Books will publish *Poets (mostly) Who Have Touched Me, Living and Dead. All True, Especially the Lies* summer of 2006. Texas Review Press will publish *Barbaro: Beyond Brokenness* in March 2008 and World Parade Books will publish *Desire* in March 2008. Red Hen will publish *Persphone* in March 2008. Coatalism Press has just published *92 Rapple Drive. Lost in the Fog* will be published by Finishing Line Press. For interviews, photographs, more bio material, reviews, interviews, prose, samples of work and more, her web site is www.lynlifshin.com.

What Others Have to Say About Lyn and Her Work...

"You might as well get used to it: Lifshin is here to stay. For men, she's sexy. For women, she's an archetype of gutsy independence. As a poet, she's nobody but herself. Frighteningly prolific and utterly intense. One of a kind."

— San Francisco Review of Books.

These poems evoke in fantasy, but with a lot of anthropological detail...Lifshin's chipped line takes on a chantlike undertone, as of native voices themselves singing from the beyond"

— New York Times Book Review

"Magnificently crafted, poems terse as needlework."

— Choice

"In sometimes fierce, uncompromising language, the poet tells what it means to be a woman in time present....An important addition for all libraries where poetry is important. Libraries are advised to get this book before it becomes a collector's item."

— Library Journal

"A modern Emily Dickinson."

— Ed Sanders

"Nightmarish snapshots, sharp visual details turned in a flash into emotional significance."

— ms magazine

"She divines moods locked inside artifacts."
— *Library Journal*

"Her poems in *Rolling Stone* stayed on my wall longer than anyone's."
— *Ken Kesey*

The 1997 Black Sparrow publication of Lyn Lifshin's selected poems, *Cold Comfort*, brought to national attention, as Small Press reviewer Len Fulton put it, "a poet of substance, range and invention," one who "everywhere roots for that stripped piece of a life—usually her own-that yields the bare emotional atom."